CW00433167

ika Cardigan in Fuchsia (143),
l (122) and Midnight (101)
ern on page 34

From left to right: Bella Jacket in Putty (121) and Fuchsia (143) pattern on page 52, Erika Cardigan in Midnight (101), Lilac Blossom (123) and Storm (102) pattern on page 22, Annika Cardigan in Storm (102), Putty (121) and Fuchsia (143) pattern on page 34, Ola Jacket in Midnight (101) pattern on page 28 and Kerstin Striped Kimono in Midnight (101), Fuchsia (143), Grass (141) and Daisy Yellow (142) pattern on page 42

Pippi Cowl in Scarlet (
pattern on page

CONTENTS

From left to right: Bella Jacket in
Putty (121) and Fuchsia (143) and
Bella Jacket in Grass (141) and
Midnight (101) pattern on page 52

From left to right: Annika Cardigan
in Storm (102), Putty (121) and
Fuchsia (143) pattern on page 34
and Ola Jacket in Midnight (101)
pattern on page 28

Erika Cardigan in Midnight (101),
Grass (141) and Fuchsia (143)
pattern on page 22

From left to right: Bella Jacket in
Putty (121) and Fuchsia (143) pattern
on page 52 and Annika Cardigan in
Storm (102), Putty (121) and Fuchsia
(143) pattern on page 34

From left to right: Pippi Cowl in
Scarlet (140) and Pippi Cowl in
Grass (141) pattern on page 48

BEFORE YOU START

Colour Coded contains 6 vibrant, bold and bright knitting patterns for adults, taking full advantage of the strong shades in the Naturally Soft Merino yarn palette. Channelling a modern, contrasting vibe the designs are striking yet versatile. These garments can be worn smart or casual, loose or tight and we try to show the different options in the photography throughout the book. Equally if brights are not your look, these designs would be stunning in more muted, sophisticated shades.

Either way we know that a hand knit will look fabulous when knitted in the right yarn and with due care paid to the process. So before you get started, please take the time to read the following basic information to help you make the most of your MillaMia pattern purchase.

TENSION / GAUGE

A standard tension is given for all the patterns in this book. As matching the tension affects the final shape and size of the item you are knitting, it can have a significant impact if it is not matched. Ensuring that you are knitting to the correct tension will result in the beautiful shape and lines of the original designs being achieved.

To check your tension we suggest that you knit a square according to the tension note at the start of each pattern (casting on an additional 10 or more stitches to the figure given in the tension note and knitting 5 to 10 more rows than specified in the tension note). You should knit the tension square in the stitch given in the note (e.g. stocking, garter, moss, etc).

Once knitted, mark out a 10cm by 10cm / 4in by 4in square using pins and count the number of stitches and rows contained within. If your tension does not quite match the one given try switching to either finer needles (if you have too few stitch in your square) or thicker needles (if you have to many stitches) until you reach the desired tension

YARN – SOME ADVICE

As there can be colour variations between dye lots when yarn is produced, we suggest that you buy all the yarn required for a project at the same time (with the same dye lot number) to ensure consistency of colour. The amount of yarn requi for each pattern is based on average requiremen meaning they are an approximate guide.

The designs in this book have been created specifically with a certain yarn composition in mind. The weight, quality, colours, comfort and finished knit effect of this yarn is ideally suited to these patterns. Substituting for another yarn ma produce a garment that is different from the design and images in this book.

SIZES

Alongside the patterns in this book we give actual measurements for the items – this shoule be used as a guide when choosing which size to knit.

Please note that where a chest measurement is giv in the table at the top of each pattern this refers to the total measurement of the garment around the chest. When the cross chest measurement is given graphically in the accompanying diagrams this is h the around chest measurement.

SKILL LEVELS

Recognising that we are not all expert knitters we have graded each pattern in the book to allow you gauge whether it is one that you feel confident to try.

USEFUL RESOURCES

believe that using quality trims with our knitwear gives the garments a professional finishing touch. Visit your local yarn/ haberdashery shop for these items and MillaMia yarn or visit www.millamia.com order yarn directly or find local stockists.

CARE OF YOUR GARMENT

See the ball band of MillaMia Naturally Soft Merino for washing and pressing instructions. Make sure you reshape your garments while they wet after washing and dry flat.

LANGUAGE

This book has been written in UK English. However, where possible, US terminology has also been included and we have provided a translation the most common knitting terms that differ between US and UK knitting conventions on page 19. Remember that when a knitting pattern refers to the left and right sides of an item it is referring to the left or right side as worn, rather than as you are looking at it.

NEED SOME HELP?

We understand that sometimes even the most experienced knitter needs a bit of advice or help on a pattern, and of course beginners cannot be expected to know everything when they start out. If you need a starting point log on to our website www.millamia.com and search through the 'Making Knitting Easy' section.

In our books do not forget to look at the Hints and Tips section for each pattern. We are constantly updating these in reprints. Based on our experience of the customer queries we have had, we try to address concerns and questions upfront with these tips.

STILL STUCK?

We check every MillaMia pattern numerous times before we go to print and pride ourselves on having a good record to date with relatively few errata.

Despite this occasionally there can be errors in knitting patterns. If you see what you think is an error the best thing is to visit www.millamia.com where any errors that have been spotted will be published under 'Pattern Revisions'. If you cannot find the answer you are looking for, then do send an email (to info@millamia.com) or contact us via the website and we will get back to you.

Bella Jacket in Putty (121) and
Fuchsia (143) pattern on page 52

ABBREVIATIONS

	alternate
prox	approximately
g	begin(ning)
nt	continue
c	decrease(ing)
	following
t	garter stitch
	increase(ing)
r K	knit
tog	knit two stitches together
	make one stitch by picking up the loop lying before the next stitch and knitting into back of it
p	make one stitch by picking up the loop lying before the next stitch and purling into back of it
hs	months
r P	purl
tog	purl two stitches together
t	pattern
so	pass slipped stitch over

pwise	purlwise
rib2 tog	rib two stitches together according to rib pattern being followed
rem	remain(ing)
rep	repeat(ing)
skpo	slip one, knit one, pass slipped stitch over – one stitch decreased
sl	slip stitch
st(s)	stitch(es)
st st	stocking stitch
tbl	through back of loop
tog	together
yf	yarn forward
yo	yarn over
yon	yarn over needle to make a st
yrn	yarn round needle
y2rn	wrap the yarn two times around needle. On the following row work into each loop separately working tbl into second loop
[ ]	work instructions within brackets as many times as directed

K AND US
NITTING TRANSLATIONS

K	US
t off	Bind off
our	Color
ey	Gray
n	Sew
ss stitch	Seed stitch
sion	Gauge
cking stitch	Stockinette stitch
n forward	Yarn over
n over needle	Yarn over
n round needle	Yarn over
n	yo2

KNITTING NEEDLE
CONVERSION CHART

Metric, mm	US size
2.75	2
3	2
3.25	3
4.5	7
5	8

m left to right: Kerstin Striped Kimono in Midnight (101), Fuchsia (143), Grass (141) and Daisy Yellow (142)
:ern on page 42, Erika Cardigan in Midnight (101), Fuchsia (143) and Grass (141) pattern on page 22, Bella Jacket
Grass (141) and Midnight (101) pattern on page 52, Ola Jacket in Midnight (101) pattern on page 28 and Annika
digan in Fuchsia (143), Petal (122) and Midnight (101) pattern on page 34

ERIKA CARDIGAN

SKILL LEVEL **Beginner**

SIZES / MEASUREMENTS
To fit bust

82	87	92	97	102	107	112	cm
32	34	36	~~38~~	(40)	42	44	in

ACTUAL MEASUREMENTS
Bust

82	89	95	102	108	114	121	cm
32	35	37 ½	40	42 ½	45	47 ½	in

Length to shoulder

72	73	74	75	76	77	78	cm
28 ¼	28 ¾	29	29 ½	30	30 ¼	30 ¾	in

Sleeve length
46cm/18in

MATERIALS
6(6:6:7:7:8:8) 50g/1 ¾oz balls of MillaMia
Naturally Soft Merino in Midnight (101) (M).
3(3:4:4:4:4:4) balls of Fuchsia (143) (A).
4(4:4:4:5:5:5) balls of Grass (141) (B).
Pair each of 3mm (US 2) and 3.25mm (US 3)
needles.
Circular 3mm (US 2) needle.

TENSION / GAUGE
25 sts and 34 rows to 10cm/4in square over st
using 3.25mm (US 3) needles.

HINTS AND TIPS
So flattering for any size – this lovely cardigan
drapes beautifully. It looks stunning in bright
colours but can equally look subdued and elegant
in softer tones. Remember to block the pockets n
and flat before you attach them. It is quite a long
fit so if you are on the short side you may wish to
adjust the final length.

ABBREVIATIONS
See page 19.

ALTERNATIVE COLOURWAYS

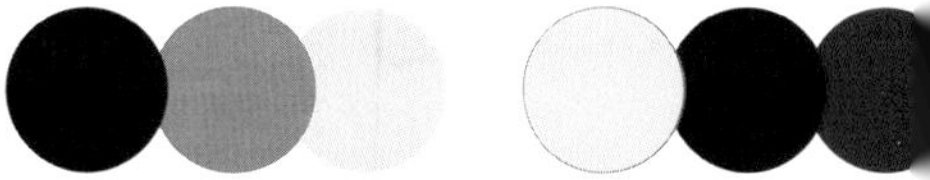

Midnight Storm Lilac	Forget Midnight Sca
101 102 Blossom	me not 101 14
123	120

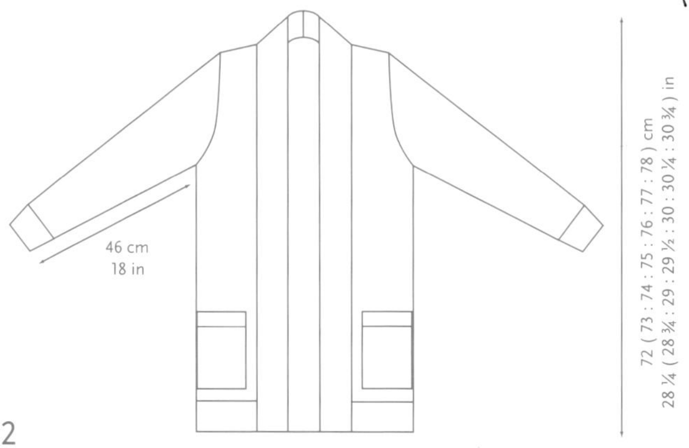

41 (44 ½ : 47 ½ : 51 : 54 : 57 : 60 ½) cm
16 (17 ½ : 18 ¾ : 20 : 21 ¼ : 22 ½ : 23 ¾) in

46 cm
18 in

72 (73 : 74 : 75 : 76 : 77 : 78) cm
28 ¼ (28 ¾ : 29 : 29 ½ : 30 : 30 ¼ : 30 ¾) in

[handwritten notes:]
M – Pink
A – Fuchsia
B – Navy

Cast on 209

BACK

With 3mm (US 2) needles and A cast on
105(113:121:129:137:145:153) sts.
1st rib row K1, [p1, k1] to end.
2nd rib row P to end.
Rep these 2 rows 13 times more.
Cut off A.
Join on M.
Change to 3.25mm (US 3) needles.
Beg with a k row work in st st until back
measures 54(54:55:55:56:56:57)cm/21 ¼(21 ¼:
21 ¾:21 ¾:22:22:22 ½)in from cast on edge,
ending with a p row.
Shape armholes
Cast off 6(7:7:8:8:9:9) sts at beg of next 2 rows.
93(99:107:113:121:127:135) sts.
Next row K3, skpo, k to last 5 sts, k2 tog, k3.
Next row P to end.
Rep the last 2 rows 6(6:7:7:8:8:9) times more.
79(85:91:97:103:109:115) sts.
Cont straight until back measures
70(71:72:73:74:75:76)cm/27 ½(28:28 ¼:28 ¾:
29 ¼:29 ½:30)in from cast on edge, ending with
a p row.
Shape back neck
Next row K22(24:26:28:30:32:34), turn and work
on these sts for first side of neck shaping.
Dec one st at neck edge on next 6 rows.
16(18:20:22:24:26:28) sts.
Work 1 row.
Shape shoulder
Next row Cast off 8(9:10:11:12:13:14) sts, k to end.
Next row P to end.
Cast off rem 8(9:10:11:12:13:14) sts.
With right side facing, cast off centre
35(37:39:41:43:45:47) sts, rejoin yarn to rem sts,
k to end.

Dec one st at neck edge on next 6 rows.
16(18:20:22:24:26:28) sts.
Work 2 rows.
Shape shoulder
Next row Cast off 8(9:10:11:12:13:14) sts, p to en
Next row K to end.
Cast off rem 8(9:10:11:12:13:14) sts.

LEFT FRONT

With 3mm (US 2) needles and A cast on
29(32:35:38:41:44:47) sts.
1st rib row K1, [p1, k1] to last 0(1:0:1:0:1:0) sts,
p0(1:0:1:0:1:0).
2nd rib row P to end.
Rep these 2 rows 13 times more.
Cut off A.
Join on M.
Change to 3.25mm (US 3) needles.
Beg with a k row work in st st until front
measures 54(54:55:55:56:56:57)cm/21 ¼(21 ¼:
21 ¾:21 ¾:22:22:22 ½)in from cast on edge,
ending with a p row.
Shape armhole
Next row Cast off 6(7:7:8:8:9:9) sts, k to end.
23(25:28:30:33:35:38) sts.
Next row P to end.
Next row K3, skpo, k to end.
Next row P to end.
Rep the last 2 rows 6(6:7:7:8:8:9) times more.
16(18:20:22:24:26:28) sts.
Cont straight until front measures same as bac
to shoulder, ending at armhole edge.
Shape shoulder
Next row Cast off 8(9:10:11:12:13:14) sts, k to e
Next row P to end.
Cast off rem 8(9:10:11:12:13:14) sts.

th 3mm (US 2) needles and A cast on
(32:35:38(41)44:47) sts.
t rib row P0(1:0:1(0)1:0), k1, [p1, k1] to end.
d rib row P to end.
p these 2 rows 13 times more.
t off A.
n on M.
ange to 3.25mm (US 3) needles.
g with a k row work in st st until front
asures 54(54:55:55(56)56:57)cm/21¼ (21¼:
¾:21¾:22:22:22½)in from cast on edge,
ding with a k row.
ape armhole
xt row Cast off 6(7:7:8(8)9:9) sts, p to end.
25:28:30(33)35:38) sts.
xt row K to last 5 sts, k2 tog, k3.
xt row P to end.
the last 2 rows 6(6:7:7(8)8:9) times more.
18:20:22(24)26:28) sts.
nt straight until front measures same as back
shoulder, ending at armhole edge.
ape shoulder
xt row Cast off 8(9:10:11(12)13:14) sts, p to end.
xt row K to end.
t off rem 8(9:10:11(12)13:14) sts.

SLEEVES

With 3mm (US 2) needles and A cast on
54(58:62:66(70)74:78) sts.
Rib row [K1, p1] to end.
Rep this row 25 times more.
Cut off A.
Join on B.
Change to 3.25mm (US 3) needles.
Beg with a k row work in st st.
Work 6 rows.
Inc row K4, m1, k to last 4 sts, m1, k4.
Work 11 rows.
Rep the last 12 rows 8 times more, and then the
inc row again. 74(78:82:86(90)94:98) sts.
Cont in st st until sleeve measures 46cm/18in
from cast on edge, ending with a p row.
Shape top
Cast off 6(7:7:8(8)9:9) sts at beg of next 2 rows.
62(64:68:70(74)76:80) sts.
Next row K1, skpo, k to last 3 sts, k2 tog, k1.
Next row P to end.
Rep the last 2 rows 10(10:11:11(12)12:13) times
more. 40(42:44:46(48)50:52) sts.
Next row K1, skpo, k to last 3 sts, k2 tog, k1.
Work 3 rows.
Rep the last 4 rows 3 times more.
32(34:36:38(40)42:44) sts.
Next row K1, skpo, k to last 3 sts, k2 tog, k1.
Next row P to end.
Rep the last 2 rows once more.
28(30:32:34(36)38:40) sts.
Cast off 3 sts at beg of next 4 rows.
Cast off.

POCKETS

With 3.25mm (US 3) needles and B cast on
27(27:29:29:31:31:33) sts.
Beg with a k row work 42(42:42:42:44:44:44)
rows in st st.
Cut off B.
Join on A.
Work 1 row.
Change to 3mm (US 2) needles.
1st rib row K1, [p1, k1] to end.
2nd rib row K to end.
Rep these 2 rows twice more, and then the 1st
rib row again.
Cast off knitwise.

LEFT NECK EDGING

Join shoulder seams.
Place a marker on centre back neck st.
With right side facing, using 3mm (US 2) circular
needle and A, starting at back neck marker, pick
up and k24(25:26:27:28:29:30) sts to shoulder
and 181(184:187:190:193:196:199) sts down left
front edge to cast on edge.
205(209:213:217:221:225:229) sts.
1st rib row K1, [p1, k1] to end.
2nd rib row K to end.
Rep these 2 rows 13 times more.
Cast off in rib.

RIGHT NECK EDGING

With right side facing, using 3mm (US 2)
circular needle and A, pick up and
k181(184:187:190:193:196:199) sts up right fro
edge to shoulder and 24(25:26:27:28:29:30) sts
to back neck marker.
205(209:213:217:221:225:229) sts.
1st rib row K1, [p1, k1] to end.
2nd rib row K to end.
Rep these 2 rows 13 times more.
Cast off in rib.

TO MAKE UP

Join neck edging seam. Join side and sleeve
seams. Sew in sleeves. Sew on pockets.

OLA JACKET

SKILL LEVEL **Improving / Experienced**

SIZES / MEASUREMENTS

To fit chest

92-97	102-107	112-117	122-127	cm
36-38	40-42	44-46	48-50	in

ACTUAL MEASUREMENTS

Chest

100	112	124	138	cm
39 ½	44	49	54 ½	in

Length to shoulder

65	67	69	71	cm
25 ½	26 ½	27 ¼	28	in

Sleeve length
50cm/19 ¾in for all sizes

MATERIALS

16(17:19:21) 50g/1 ¾oz balls of MillaMia
Naturally Soft Merino in Midnight (101).
Pair each of 3mm (US 2) and 3.25mm (US 3)
knitting needles.
19 buttons (approx 15mm/⅝ in diameter).

TENSION / GAUGE

25 sts and 34 rows to 10cm/4in square over st
using 3.25mm (US 3) needles.

HINTS AND TIPS

A slouchy, relaxed fit, this garment actually look
great on women too (as you can see on the
inside back cover of the Colour Coded book!).
The short row shaping in the collar is included
the instructions to give a bit of lift to the back o
the collar.

ABBREVIATIONS

See page 19.

ALTERNATIVE COLOURWAYS

Storm	Seaside	Scarlet	Fawn
102	161	140	160

50 (56 : 62 : 69) cm
19 ¾ (22 : 24 ½ : 27 ¼) in

65 (67 : 69 : 71) cm
25 ½ (26 ½ : 27 ¼ : 28) in

50 cm
19 ¾ in

BACK

With 3mm (US 2) needles cast on
126(142:158:174) sts.
1st row P2, [k2, p2] to end.
2nd row P to end.
Rep the last 2 rows 9 times more.
Change to 3.25mm (US 3) needles.
Beg with a k row, work in st st until back
measures 43(44:45:46)cm/17(17 ¼:17 ¾:18)in
from cast on edge, ending with a p row.
Shape armholes
Cast off 8(9:10:11) sts at beg of next 2 rows.
110(124:138:152) sts.
Next row K2, skpo, k to last 4 sts, k2 tog, k2.
Next row P to end.
Rep the last 2 rows 7(9:11:13) times more.
94(104:114:124) sts.
Cont straight until back measures 65(67:69:71)cm/
25 ½(26 ½ :27 ¼:28)in.
Shape shoulders
Cast off 9(10:11:12) sts at beg of next 6 rows.
Leave rem 40(44:48:52) sts on a holder.

RIGHT FRONT

With 3mm (US 2) needles cast on 74(82:90:98) sts.
1st row P2, [k2, p2] to end.
2nd row P to end.
Rep the last 2 rows 9 times more.
Change to 3.25mm (US 3) needles.
Next row (right side) P2, [k2, p2] 7 times,
k44(52:60:68).
Next row P to end.
These 2 rows form the st st with rib border.
Work straight until front measures 43(44:45:46)cm/
17(17 ¼:17 ¾:18)in from cast on edge, ending
with a right side row.

Shape armhole
Cast off 8(9:10:11) sts at beg of next row.
66(73:80:87) sts.
Next row Patt to last 4 sts, k2 tog, k2.
Next row Patt to end.
Rep the last 2 rows 7(9:11:13) times more.
58(63:68:73) sts.
Work straight until front measures 55(56:56:57)cm
21 ½(22:22:22 ½)in from cast on edge, ending
with a wrong side row.
Shape neck
Next row Cast off 19(20:21:22) sts, patt to end.
39(43:47:51) sts.
Next row Patt to end.
Next row Skpo, patt to end.
Rep the last 2 rows until 27(30:33:36) sts rem.
Cont straight until front measures same as bac
to shoulder, ending at armhole edge.
Shape shoulder
Cast off 9(10:11:12) sts at beg of next and foll
wrong side row.
Work 1 row.
Cast off rem 9(10:11:12) sts.
Mark positions for 6 pairs of buttons, the first
2.5cm/1in from cast on edge, the sixth 3cm/
1 ¼in from neck edge and the rem 4 spaced
evenly between.

LEFT FRONT

With 3mm (US 2) needles cast on 74(82:90:98) st
1st row P2, [k2, p2] to end.
2nd row P to end.
Rep the last 2 rows 3 times more.
1st buttonhole row Rib to last 27 sts, work2 to
y2rn, work2 tog, rib 16, work2 tog, y2rn,
work2 tog, rib 3.
2nd buttonhole row Rib to end, working twice
into y2rn on previous row.

rk a further 10 rows.
ange to 3.25mm (US 3) needles.
xt row (right side) K44(52:60:68), p2, [k2, p2]
mes.
xt row P to end.
ese 2 rows form the st st with rib border.
rk rem buttonholes as before to match
rkers.
rk straight until front measures 43(44:45:46)cm/
17 ¼:17 ¾:18)in from cast on edge, ending
h a wrong side row.
pe armhole
st off 8(9:10:11) sts at beg of next row.
73:80:87) sts.
xt row Patt to end.
xt row K2, skpo, patt to end.
xt row Patt to end.
the last 2 rows 7(9:11:13) times more.
63:68:73) sts.
rk straight until front measures 55(56:56:57)cm/
½(22:22:22 ½)in from cast on edge, ending
h a right side row.
pe neck
xt row Cast off 19(20:21:22) sts, patt to end.
43:47:51) sts.
xt row Patt to last 4 sts, k2 tog, k2.
xt row Patt to end.
the last 2 rows until 27(30:33:36) sts rem.
t straight until front measures same as back
houlder, ending at armhole edge.
pe shoulder
t off 9(10:11:12) sts at beg of next and foll
t side row.
k 1 row.
t off rem 9(10:11:12) sts.

SLEEVES

With 3mm (US 2) needles, cast on 66(74:82:90) sts.
1st row K2, [p2, k2] to end.
2nd row P2, [k2, p2] to end.
Rep the last 2 rows 9 times more.
Change to 3.25mm (US 3) needles.
Beg with a k row, work in st st.
Work 4 rows.
1st inc row K3, m1, k to last 3 sts, m1, k3.
Work 6 rows.
2nd inc row P3, m1p, p to last 3 sts, m1p, p3.
Work 6 rows.
Rep the last 14 rows 9 times more, and then the
1st inc row again. 108(116:124:132) sts.
Cont straight until sleeve measures 50cm/19 ¾in
from cast on edge, ending with a p row.
Shape top
Cast off 8(9:10:11) sts at beg of next 2 rows.
92(98:104:110) sts.
Next row K2, skpo, k to last 4 sts, k2 tog, k2.
Next row P to end.
Rep the last 2 rows 7(8:9:10) times more.
76(80:84:88) sts.
Next row K2, skpo, k to last 4 sts, k2 tog, k2.
Next row P to end.
Next row K to end.
Next row P to end.
Rep the last 4 rows 3 times more. 68(72:76:80) sts.
Cast off 4 sts at beg of next 12 rows.
Cast off.

POCKETS (make 2)

With 3.25mm (US 3) needles, cast on
40(40:46:46) sts.
Beg with a k row, work 55(57:59:61) rows in st st.
Pocket top
1st row P1, [k2, p1] to end.

2nd row P to end.
Rep the last 2 rows 7 times more.
Next row (buttonhole row) Rib 18(18:21:21),
p2 tog, y2rn, p2 tog, rib 18(18:21:21).
Next row P to end, working twice into y2rn on
previous row.
Work a further 6 rows.
Cast off in rib.

NECKBAND

Join shoulder seams.
With 3mm (US 2) needles, cast on 14 sts.
1st row P2, [k2, p2] 3 times.
2nd row P to end.
Rep the last 2 rows once more.
Next row (buttonhole row) P2, k2, p1, p2 tog,
y2rn, p2 tog, p1, k2, p2.
Next row P to end, working twice into y2rn on
previous row.
Work a further 238(246:254:262) rows in patt.
Cast off in patt.
With buttonhole to left side, sew around neck edge.

COLLAR

With wrong side of neckband facing, using 3mm
(US 2) needles, pick up and k102(106:110:114) sts
between first and last 20(22:24:26) rows of
neckband.
1st row K2, [p2, k2] to end.
2nd row K to end.
These 2 rows set the rib.
Next 2 rows Patt to last 24 sts, turn.
Next 2 rows Patt to last 16 sts, turn.
Next 2 rows Patt to last 8 sts, turn.
Next row Patt to end.
Change to 3.25mm (US 3) needles.

Cont in rib patt until collar measures 8cm/3in
along short edge, ending with a first row.
Cast off.

EPAULETTES (make 2)

With 3mm (US 2) needles, cast on 10 sts.
1st row P2, [k2, p2] twice.
2nd row P to end.
Rep the last 2 rows once more.
Next row (buttonhole row) P2, k1, k2 tog, y2rn,
skpo, k1, p2.
Next row P to end, working twice into y2rn on
previous row.
Work a further 24 rows in patt.
Cast off in patt.

WRIST STRAPS (make 2)

With 3mm (US 2) needles, cast on 10 sts.
1st row P2, [k2, p2] twice.
2nd row P to end.
Rep the last 2 rows once more.
Next row (buttonhole row) P2, k1, k2 tog, y2rn
skpo, k1, p2.
Next row P to end, working twice into y2rn on
previous row.
Work a further 44 rows in patt.
Cast off in patt.

TO MAKE UP

Join side and sleeve seams. Sew in sleeves.
Sew on epaulettes. Sew on st st only section o
pockets, folding rib onto right side. Sew cast o
edge of wrist straps to underarm seams appro
9cm/3 ½in above cuff edge. Sew on buttons.

ANNIKA CARDIGAN

SKILL LEVEL **Improving**

SIZES / MEASUREMENTS
To fit bust

82	87	92	97	102	107	112	cm
32	34	36	38	40	42	44	in

ACTUAL MEASUREMENTS
Bust

82	88	94	100	107	114	120	cm
32	34 ½	37	39 ¾	42	45	47 ¼	in

Length to shoulder

65	66	67	68	69	70	71	cm
25 ½	26	26 ½	26 ¾	27 ¼	27 ½	28	in

Sleeve length
39cm/15 ½in

MATERIALS
8(8:9:9:10:10:11) 50g/1 ¾oz balls of MillaMia
Naturally Soft Merino in Storm (102) (A).
6(6:7:7:8:8) balls of Putty (121) (B).
3 balls of Fuchsia (143) (C).
Pair each of 3mm (US 2) and 3.25mm (US 3) needles.
Circular 3.25mm (US 3) needle.
Three buttons (approx 21mm/¾in diameter).

TENSION / GAUGE
25 sts and 34 rows to 10cm/4in square over st
using 3.25mm (US 3) needles.

HINTS AND TIPS
This cardigan can be worn oversized and slouc
If you make a larger size you could even belt it
a kimono, wrap style. It is a wide, flared fit so a
smaller size than normal may be more suitable
if you want a less casual style. The pockets are
optional – see our second colourway image for
how it looks without pockets too. Even though
circular needles are specified you are still work
back and forth in rows, not in the round. The
circular needles are simply used to accommod
the number of stitches cast on.

ABBREVIATIONS
See page 19.

ALTERNATIVE COLOURWAYS

Fuchsia	Petal	Midnight		Fawn	Snow	Plu
143	122	101		160	124	16.

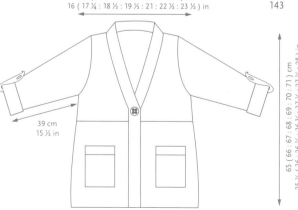

41 (44 : 47 : 50 : 53 ½ : 57 : 60) cm
16 (17 ¼ : 18 ½ : 19 ½ : 21 : 22 ½ : 23 ½) in

39 cm
15 ½ in

65 (66 : 67 : 68 : 69 : 70 : 71) cm
25 ½ (26 : 26 ½ : 26 ¾ : 27 ¼ : 27 ½ : 28) in

1A A 30 + T67 7 80 + 16
354

BACK

With 3.25mm (US 3) circular needle and A cast
on 127(137:147(157)167:177:187) sts.
Work backwards and forwards in rows.
1st row in g-st is a wrong side row.
Cont in g-st until back measures
32(32:33:(33)34:34:35)cm/12 ½(12 ½:13:13:13 ½:
13 ½:13 ¾)in from cast on edge, ending with a
right side row.
Dec row K7, [k2 tog, k3] 22(24:26(28)30:32:34)
times, k2 tog, k8.
104(112:120(128)136:144:152) sts.
Change to B.
Beg with a k row cont in st st until back measures
47(47:48(48)49:49:50)cm/18 ½(18 ½:19:19:19 ¼:
19 ¼:19 ¾)in from cast on edge, ending with a
p row.
Shape armholes
Cast off 6(7:7(8)8:9:9) sts at beg of next 2 rows.
92(98:106(112)120:126:134) sts.
Next row K3, skpo, k to last 5 sts, k2 tog, k3.
Next row P to end.
Rep the last 2 rows 6(6:7(7)8:8:9) times more.
78(84:90:96)102:108:114) sts.
Cont straight until back measures
63(64:65(66)67:68:69)cm/24 ¾(25 ¼:25 ¾:26:26 ½:
26 ¾:27 ¼)in from cast on edge, ending with a p row.
Shape back neck
Next row K22(24:26(28)30:32:34), turn and work
on these sts for first side of neck shaping.
Dec one st at neck edge on next 4 rows.
18(20:22(24)26:28:30) sts.
Work 1 row.
Shape shoulder
Next row Cast off 9(10:11(12)13:14:15) sts, k to end.
Next row P to end.
Cast off rem 9(10:11(12)13:14:15) sts.
With right side facing, rejoin yarn to rem sts, cast

off centre 34(36:38(40)42:44:46) sts, k to end.
Dec one st at neck edge on next 4 rows.
18(20:22:(24)26:28:30) sts.
Work 2 rows.
Shape shoulder
Next row Cast off 9(10:(11)12:13:14:15) sts, p to end.
Next row K to end.
Cast off rem 9(10:11(12)13:14:15) sts.

LEFT FRONT

With 3.25mm (US 3) needles and A cast on
60(65:70(75)80:85:90) sts.
Cont in g-st until front measures
32(32:33:33:34:34:35)cm/12 ½(12 ½:13:13:13 ½
13 ½:13 ¾)in from cast on edge, ending with a
right side row.
Dec row K1, [k2 tog, k3] 11(12:13(14)15:16:17)
times, k2 tog, k2.
48(52:56(60)64:68:72) sts.
Change to B and st st.
Shape front neck
1st row K to last 4 sts, k2 tog, k2.
Work 3 rows.
Dec one st at neck edge on the next and
11(12:13(14)15:16:17) foll 4th rows and 4 foll
6th rows **at the same time** when front measure
47(47:48(48)49:49:50)cm/18 ½(18 ½:19:19:19 ¼
19 ¼:19 ¾)in from cast on edge, ending with a
wrong side row, shape armhole as follows:
Shape armhole
Next row Cast off 6(7:7(8)8:9:9) sts, work to en
Next row P to end.
Next row K2, skpo, work to end.
Next row P to end.
Dec one st at armhole edge on next 6(6:7(7)8:8:8
right side rows.
When all neck decs have been worked cont
straight until front measures the same as back
shoulder shaping, ending at armhole edge.

36

Shape shoulder
Next row Cast off 9(10:11:12:13:14:15) sts, k to end.
P 1 row.
Cast off rem 9(10:11:12:13:14:15) sts.

RIGHT FRONT

With 3.25mm (US 3) needles and A cast on
60(65:70:75:80:85:90) sts.
Cont in g-st until front measures
32(32:33:33:34:34:35)cm/12 ½(12 ½:13:13:13 ½:
13 ½:13 ¾)in from cast on edge, ending with a
right side row.
Dec row K2, [k2 tog, k3] 11(12:13:14:15:16:17)
times, k2 tog, k1.
48(52:56:60:64:68:72) sts.
Change to B and st st.   — Button hole
Shape front neck
1st row K2, skpo, k to end.
Work 3 rows.
Dec one st at neck edge on the next and
11(12:13:14:15:16:17) foll 4th rows and 4 foll
6th rows **at the same time** when front measures
47(47:48:48:49:49:50)cm/18 ½(18 ½:19:19:19 ¼:
19 ¼:19 ¾)in from cast on edge, ending with a
right side row, shape armhole as follows:
Shape armhole   Dure
Next row Cast off 6(7:7:8:8:9:9) sts, work to end.
Next row K to last 4 sts, k2 tog, k2.
Next row P to end.
Dec one st at armhole edge on next 6(6:7:7:8:8:9)
right side rows.
When all neck decs have been worked cont
straight until front measures the same as back to
shoulder shaping, ending at armhole edge.
Shape shoulder
Next row Cast off 9(10:11:12:13:14:15) sts, p to end.
K 1 row.
Cast off rem 9(10:11:12:13:14:15) sts.

POCKETS (make 2 - optional)

With 3.25mm (US 3) needles and A cast on
32(32:32:36:36:36:36) sts.
Beg with a k row work 10(10:10:11:11:11:11)cm
4(4:4:4 ¼:4 ¼:4 ¼:4 ¼)in in g-st, ending with a
wrong side row.
Change to C.
K 1 row.
Next row P to end.
Next row K3, [p2, k2] to last 5 sts, p2, k3.
Rep the last 2 rows 4 times more, and then the
first row again.
Cast off in rib.

SLEEVES

With 3mm (US 2) needles and A cast on
74(78:82:86:90:94:98) sts.
Cont in g-st until cuff measures 10cm/4in from
cast on edge, ending with a wrong side row.
Change to B.
Mark each end of last row with a coloured thread.
Beg with a k row cont in st st until sleeve
measures 12cm/4 ¾in from coloured thread,
ending with a p row.
Change to 3.25mm (US 3) needles.
Beg with a k row work in st st until sleeve
measures 34cm/13 ½in from coloured thread,
ending with a p row.
Shape top
Cast off 6(7:7:8:8:9:9) sts at beg of next 2 rows.
62(64:68:70:74:76:80) sts.
Next row K1, skpo, k to last 3 sts, k2 tog, k1.
Next row P to end.
Rep the last 2 rows 8(8:9:9:10:10:11) times mo
44(46:48:50:52:54:56) sts.
Next row K1, skpo, k to last 3 sts, k2 tog, k1.
Work 3 rows.

Rep the last 4 rows 5 times more.
32(34:36:38:40:42:44) sts.
Next row K1, skpo, k to last 3 sts, k2 tog, k1.
Next row P to end.
Rep the last 2 rows once more.
28(30:32:34:36:38:40) sts.
Cast off 3 sts at beg of next 4 rows.
Cast off.

FRONTBAND

With 3mm (US 2) needles and C cast on 16 sts.
1st row [P1, k2] 4 times, p1, k3.
2nd row P to end.
Rep the last 2 rows until band, when slightly
stretched fits up right front to beg of neck
shaping, ending with a p row.
Buttonhole row P1, k2, p1, k2, p2 tog, y2rn, skpo,
k2, p1, k3.
Next row P to end, working twice into y2rn on
previous row.
Cont in patt until band fits up remainder of right
front across back neck and down left front.
Cast off.

SLEEVE BANDS (make 2)

With 3mm (US 2) needles and C cast on 13 sts
1st row P1, [k2, p1] 4 times.
2nd row P to end.
Rep the last 2 rows until band measures 18cm/7
from cast on edge, ending with a p row.
Cast off in rib.

TO MAKE UP

Join side and sleeve seams. Sew on sleeves,
reversing seam on g-st to fold back. Sew on
pockets (if using). Fold cuff in half onto right
side, place sleeve bands around cuff on sleeves
and secure in place with a button. Sew on front
button.

KERSTIN STRIPED KIMON

SKILL LEVEL **Beginner / Improving**

SIZES / MEASUREMENTS

To fit bust

82	87	92	97	102	107	112	cm
32	34	36	38	40	42	44	in

ACTUAL MEASUREMENTS

Bust

87	93	100	106	113	119	125	cm
34	36 ½	39 ½	41 ¾	44 ½	47	49	in

Length to shoulder

62	64	65 ½	67	68 ½	70 ½	72	cm
24 ½	25	25 ¾	26 ½	27	27 ¾	28 ½	in

Sleeve length

45	45	46	46	46	47	47	cm
17 ¾	17 ¾	18	18	18	18 ½	18 ½	in

MATERIALS

10(11:11:12:13:13:14) 50g/1 ¾oz balls of MillaMia
Naturally Soft Merino in Midnight (101) (M).
1(2:2:2:2:3:3) balls of Fuchsia (143) (A).
1(1:1:1:2:2:2) balls of Grass (141) (B).
One ball of Daisy Yellow (142) (C).
Pair each of 3mm (US 2) and 3.25mm (US 3)
knitting needles.
3mm (US 2) and 3.25mm (US 3) circular needles.
5 small buttons (approx 12mm/½in diameter).
1 small popper (snap fastener) button.

TENSION / GAUGE

25 sts and 34 rows to 10cm/4in square over st
using 3.25mm (US 3) needles.

HINTS AND TIPS

A nice simple knit, the asymmetric opening
results in a kimono style shape. It is quite a
large, loose fit on the body so look carefully
at the actual measurements to decide which
size to knit. We suggest adding a popper-style
jigger button (a functional but not visible inne
button) to keep the item partly closed and to
achieve a leaner, more streamlined look. Circu
needles are used to accommodate the numbe
stitches, you still work back and forth in rows.

ABBREVIATIONS

See also page 19.

ALTERNATIVE COLOURWAYS

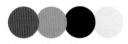

Storm	Plum	Claret	Forget me not	Snow	Scarlet	Midnight	F
102	162	102	120	124	140	101	

43 ½ (46 ½ : 50 : 53 : 56 ½ : 59 ½ : 62 ½) cm
17 (18 ¼ : 19 ¾ : 20 ¾ : 22 ¼ : 23 ½ : 24 ½) in

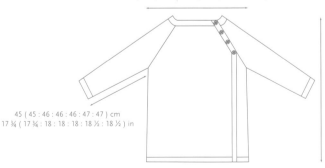

45 (45 : 46 : 46 : 46 : 47 : 47) cm
17 ¾ (17 ¾ : 18 : 18 : 18 : 18 ½ : 18 ½) in

BACK

With 3mm (US 2) circular needle and M cast on
135(143:151:159:167:175:183) sts.
Work backwards and forwards in rows.
1st, 3rd, 5th and 7th sizes only
1st row P1, [k1, p1] to end.
2nd row K1, [p1, k1] to end.
2nd, 4th and 6th sizes only
1st row K1, [p1, k1] to end.
2nd row P1, [k1, p1] to end.
All sizes
Rep the last 2 rows twice more.
Change to 3.25mm (US 3) circular needle.
Beg with a k row cont in st st.
Work 6 rows.
Dec row K4, skpo, k to last 6 sts, k2 tog, k4.
Work 9 rows.
Rep the last 10 rows 10 times more, and then the
dec row again.
111(119:127:135:143:151:159) sts.
Work straight until back measures 41cm/16 ¼in
from cast on edge, ending with a p row.
Shape raglan armholes
Working in stripes of 2(6:10:14:18:22:26) rows M,
8 rows A, 2 rows M, 4 rows B, 2 rows M, 2 rows
C, 2 rows M, 6 rows A, 2 rows M, 4 rows B,
2 rows M, 2 rows C, 2 rows M, 8 rows A, 2 rows
M, 2 rows B, 2 rows M, 2 rows A.
Cast off 5(6:7:8:9:10:11) sts at beg of next 2 rows.
101(107:113:119:125:131:137) sts.
Next row K2, skpo, k to last 4 sts, k2 tog, k2.
Next row P to end.
Rep the last 2 rows 26(28:30:32:34:36:38) times
more.
47(49:51:53:55:57:59) sts.
Leave these sts on a holder.

SLEEVES

With 3mm (US 2) needles and M cast on
54(58:62:66:72:76:80) sts.
Rib row [K1, p1] to end.
Rep the last row 7 times more.
Change to 3.25mm (US 3) needles.
Beg with a k row cont in st st.
Work 16(4:12:8:8:8:4) rows.
Inc row K4, m1, k to last 4 sts, m1, k4.
Work 13(13:11:11:9:9:9) rows.
Rep the last 14(14:12:12:10:10:10) rows
7(8:9:10:10:11:12) times more, and then the in
row again. 72(78:84:90:96:102:108) sts.
Cont straight until sleeve measures
45(45:46:46:46:47:47)cm/17 ¾(17 ¾:18:18:18:18
18 ½)in from cast on edge, ending with a p row.
Shape raglans
Working in stripes of 2(6:10:14:18:22:26) rows
8 rows A, 2 rows M, 4 rows B, 2 rows M, 2 row
C, 2 rows M, 6 rows A, 2 rows M, 4 rows B,
2 rows M, 2 rows C, 2 rows M, 8 rows A, 2 row
M, 2 rows B, 2 rows M, 2 rows A.
Cast off 5(6:7:8:9:10:11) sts at beg of next 2 ro
62(66:70:74:78:82:86) sts.
Next row K2, skpo, k to last 4 sts, k2 tog, k2.
Next row P to end.
Next row K to end.
Next row P to end.
Rep the last 4 rows 9(10:11:12:13:14:15) times
more.
42(44:46:48:50:52:54) sts.
Next row K2, skpo, k to last 4 sts, k2 tog, k2.
Next row P to end.
Rep the last 2 rows 6 times more.
28(30:32:34:36:38:40) sts.
Leave these sts on a holder.

EFT FRONT

ith 3mm (US 2) needles and M cast on
(51:54:57:60:63:66) sts.
t row P0(1:0:1:0:1:0), [k1, p1] to end.
d row [K1, p1] to last 0(1:0:1:0:1:0) sts,
(1:0:1:0:1:0).
p the last 2 rows twice more.
ange to 3.25mm (US 3) needles.
g with a k row cont in st st.
ork 6 rows.
c row K4, skpo, k to end.
ork 9 rows.
p the last 10 rows 10 times more, and then the
c row again.
(39:42:45:48:51:54) sts.
ork straight until front measures 41cm/16 ¼in
m cast on edge, ending with a p row.
ape raglan armhole
orking in stripes of 2(6:10:14:18:22:26) rows M,
ows A, 2 rows M, 4 rows B, 2 rows M, 2 rows
2 rows M, 6 rows A, 2 rows M, 4 rows B,
ows M, 2 rows C, 2 rows M, 8 rows A, 2 rows
2 rows B, 2 rows M, 2 rows A.
xt row Cast off 5(6:7:8:9:10:11) sts, k to end.
(33:35:37:39:41:43) sts.
xt row P to end.
xt row K2, skpo, k to end.
xt row P to end.
p the last 2 rows 26(28:30:32:34:36:38) times
re. 4 sts.
ave these sts on a holder.

RIGHT FRONT

With 3mm (US 2) circular needle and M cast on
112(117:122:127:132:137:142) sts.
Work backwards and forwards in rows.
1st row P1, [k1, p1] to last 1(0:1:0:1:0:1) sts,
k1(0:1:0:1:0:1).
2nd row P1(0:1:0:1:0:1), [k1, p1] to last st, k1.
Rep the last 2 rows twice more.
Change to 3.25mm (US 3) circular needle.
Beg with a k row cont in st st.
Work 6 rows.
Dec row K to last 6 sts, k2 tog, k4.
Work 9 rows.
Rep the last 10 rows 10 times more, and then the
dec row again.
100(105:110:115:120:125:130) sts.
Work straight until front measures 41cm/16 ¼in
from cast on edge, ending with a k row.
Shape raglan armhole
Working in stripes of 1(5:9:13:17:21:25) rows M,
8 rows A, 2 rows M, 4 rows B, 2 rows M, 2 rows
C, 2 rows M, 6 rows A, 2 rows M, 4 rows B,
2 rows M, 2 rows C, 2 rows M, 8 rows A, 2 rows
M, 2 rows B, 2 rows M, 2 rows A.
Next row Cast off 5(6:7:8:9:10:11) sts, p to end.
95(99:103:107:111:115:119) sts.
Next row K to last 4 sts, k2 tog, k2.
Next row P to end.
Rep the last 2 rows 4(6:8:10:12:14:16) times
more. 90(92:94:96:98:100:102) sts.
Next row K2, skpo, k to last 4 sts, k2 tog, k2.
Next row P to end.
Rep the last 2 rows 21 times more.
46(48:50:52:54:56:58) sts.
Leave these sts on a holder.

NECKBAND

With right side facing using 3mm (US 2) circular needle and M, k45(47:49:51:53:55:57) across right front, k last st tog with first st of right sleeve, k26(28:30:32:34:36:38), k last st of right sleeve tog with first st of back, k45(47:49:51:53:55:57) sts, k last st tog with first st of left sleeve, k26(28:30:32:34:36:38), k last st of left sleeve tog with first st of left front, k3. 149(157:165:173:181:189:197) sts.
1st row K1, [p1, k1] to end.
2nd row P1, [k1, p1] to end.
Rep the last 2 rows once more, and then the first row again.
Cast off in rib.

LEFT FRONT BAND

Using 3mm (US 2) circular needle and M pick up and k177(179:181:185:187:189:191) sts along left front edge.
1st row K1, [p1, k1] to end.
2nd row P1, [k1, p1] to end.
Buttonhole row Rib to last 4 sts, yrn, k2 tog, p1, k1.
Rib 2 rows.
Cast off in rib.

RIGHT FRONT BAND

Using 3mm (US 2) circular needle and M pick up and k177(179:181:185:187:189:191) sts along right front edge.
1st row K1, [p1, k1] to end.
2nd row P1, [k1, p1] to end.
Buttonhole row Rib 2, yrn, work2 tog, [rib 10, yrn work2 tog] 3 times, rib to end.
Rib 2 rows.
Cast off in rib.

TO MAKE UP

Join raglan seams. Join side and sleeve seams. Sew on buttons. Place one half of popper button on the inside of the right side button band halfway between the hem and the lowest sewn button, with the other half of the popper button on the left front band.

PIPPI COWL

SKILL LEVEL **Improving**

SIZES / MEASUREMENTS
One size measuring 120cm/47in long by 20cm/
8in wide.

MATERIALS
Five 50g/1 ¾oz balls of MillaMia Naturally Soft
Merino in Grass (141).
3.25mm (US 3) circular needle.
Stitch marker.

TENSION / GAUGE
25 sts and 42 rounds to 10cm/4in square
over drop stitch pattern using 3.25mm (US 3)
needles.

HINTS AND TIPS
This unisex cowl is knitted in the round on a
circular needle. Be sure to check that your stitches
are not twisted before joining your cast on
stitches. The 7 round pattern is easily memorised
and grows really quickly. Alternatively you can of
course knit the pattern flat and then seam the row
ends to make the cowl shape if you prefer – however
remember then to use just knit rows to create garter
stitch as the pattern is a garter drop stitch.

ABBREVIATIONS
See page 19.

ALTERNATIVE COLOURWAYS

Scarlet	Daisy	Fuchsia	Peacoc
140	Yellow	143	144
	142		

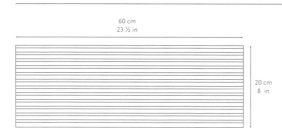

60 cm
23 ½ in

20 cm
8 in

TO MAKE

Using 3.25mm (US 3) circular needle cast on
300 sts and join for knitting in the round (being
careful not to twist your sts).
Place a stitch marker to mark the beginning of the
round.
Round 1 K.
Round 2 P.
Round 3 K.
Round 4 P.
Round 5 *K1 winding yarn twice round needle;
rep from * to end.
Round 6 K to end dropping the extra loops.
Round 7 P.
These 7 rounds form the drop st patt and are rep
throughout.
Cont working the patt 11 times more, for a total
of 12 patt reps (84 rounds in total).
Next round K.
Next round P.
Next round K.
Cast off loosely pwise.

FINISHING

Weave in ends and block lightly to
measurements.

BELLA JACKET

SKILL LEVEL **Beginner / Improving**

SIZES / MEASUREMENTS
To fit bust

82	87	92	97	102	107	112	cm
32	34	36	38	40	42	44	in

ACTUAL MEASUREMENTS
Bust

82	88	94	101	107	114	120	cm
32	34 ½	37	39 ¾	42	45	47 ¼	in

Length to shoulder

50	51	52	53	54	55	56	cm
19 ¾	20	20 ½	20 ¾	21 ¼	21 ¾	22	in

Sleeve length
34cm/13 ½in

MATERIALS
8(9:10:11:12:13:14) 50g/1 ¾oz balls of MillaMia
Naturally Soft Merino in Putty (101) (M).
4(4:5:5:5:5:6) balls of Fuchsia (143) (C).
Pair each of 3mm (US 2) and 3.25mm (US 3)
needles.
Circular 3mm (US 2) and 3.25mm (US 3)
needles.
Two buttons (approx 18mm/¾in diameter).

TENSION / GAUGE
25 sts and 34 rows to 10cm/4in square over st
using 3.25mm (US 3) needles.

HINTS AND TIPS
Even though circular needles are used for
this pattern, please note you are still working
backwards and forwards in rows - not in
the round. The circular needles are used to
accommodate the large number of stitches cas
on. If you feel that you can fit all the stitches
comfortably on straight needles you can of
course simply use these instead.

ABBREVIATIONS
See page 19.

ALTERNATIVE COLOURWAYS

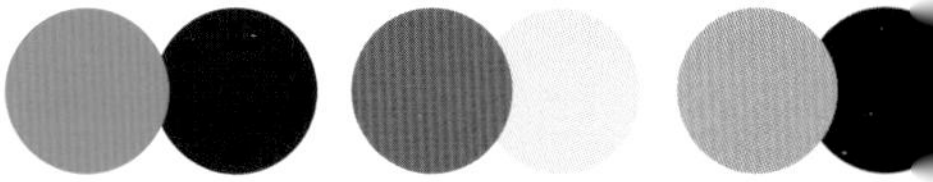

Grass	Midnight	Storm	Lilac	Plum	Clar
141	101	102	Blossom	162	104
			123		

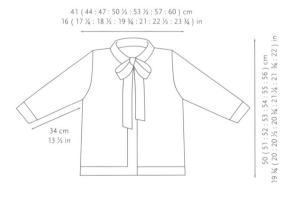

41 (44 : 47 : 50 ½ : 53 ½ : 57 : 60) cm
16 (17 ¼ : 18 ½ : 19 ¾ : 21 : 22 ½ : 23 ¾) in

34 cm
13 ½ in

50 (51 : 52 : 53 : 54 : 55 : 56) cm
19 ¾ (20 : 20 ½ : 20 ¾ : 21 ¼ : 21 ¾ : 22) in

BACK

With 3mm (US 2) circular needle and C cast on
117(125:133:141:149:157:165) sts.
Work backwards and forwards in rows.
Moss st row K1, [p1, k1] to end.
Rep the last row 13 times more, inc one st at
centre of last row.
118(126:134:142:150:158:166) sts.
Cut off C.
Join on M.
Change to 3.25mm (US 3) circular needle.
Beg with a k row work in st st.
Work 12 rows.
Dec row K5, skpo, k to last 7 sts, k2 tog, k5.
Work 11 rows.
Rep the last 12 rows 5 times more, and then the
dec row again.
104(112:120:128:136:144:152) sts.
Work straight until back measures
32(32:33:33:34:34:35)cm/12 ½(12 ½:13:13:13 ½:
13 ½:13 ¾)in from cast on edge, ending with a p row.
Shape armholes
Cast off 4(5:5:6:6:7:7) sts at beg of next 2 rows.
96(102:110:116:124:130:138) sts.
Next row K3, skpo, k to last 5 sts, k2 tog, k3.
Next row P to end.
Rep the last 2 rows 3(3:4:4:5:5:6) times more.
88(94:100:106:112:118:124) sts.
Cont straight until back measures
48(49:50:51:52:53:54)cm/19(19 ¼:19 ¾:20:20 ½:
21:21 ¼)in from cast on edge, ending with a p
row.
Shape back neck
Next row K27(29:31:33:35:37:39), turn and work
on these sts for first side of neck shaping.
Dec one st at neck edge on next 4 rows.
23(25:27:29:31:33:35) sts.
Work 1 row.

Shape shoulder
Next row Cast off 11(12:13:14:15:16:17) sts, k to en
Next row P to end.
Cast off rem 12(13:14:15:16:17:18) sts.
With right side facing, slip centre
34(36:38:40:42:44:46) sts onto a holder, rejoin
yarn to rem sts, k to end.
Dec one st at neck edge on next 4 rows.
23(25:27:29:31:33:35) sts.
Work 2 rows.
Shape shoulder
Next row Cast off 11(12:13:14:15:16:17) sts, p to er
Next row K to end.
Cast off rem 12(13:14:15:16:17:18) sts.

LEFT FRONT

With 3mm (US 2) needles and C cast on
55(59:63:67:71:75:79) sts.
Moss st row K1, [p1, k1] to end.
Rep the last row 13 times more.
Cut off C.
Join on M.
Change to 3.25mm (US 3) needles.
Beg with a k row work in st st.
Work 12 rows.
Dec row K5, skpo, k to end.
Work 11 rows.
Rep the last 12 rows 5 times more, and then th
dec row again. 48(52:56:60:64:68:72) sts.
Work straight until front measures
32(32:33:33:34:34:35)cm/12 ½(12 ½:13:13:13 ½
13 ½:13 ¾)in from cast on edge, ending with
a p row.
Shape armhole
Next row Cast off 4(5:5:6:6:7:7) sts, k to end.
44(47:51:54:58:61:65) sts.
Next row P to end.
Next row K3, skpo, k to end.

Next row P to end.

Rep the last 2 rows 3(3:4:4:5:5:6) times more. 40(43:46:49:52:55:58) sts.

Cont straight until front measures 42(42:43:43:44:44:45)cm/16½(16½:17:17:17¼:17¼: 17½)in from cast on edge, ending with a p row.

Shape neck

Next row K to last 4 sts, k2 tog, k2.

Next row P2, p2 tog, p to end.

Rep the last 2 rows until 23(25:27:29:31:33:35) sts rem.

Work straight until front measures the same as back to shoulder, ending at armhole edge.

Shape shoulder

Next row Cast off 11(12:13:14:15:16:17) sts, k to end.

Next row P to end.

Cast off rem 12(13:14:15:16:17:18) sts.

RIGHT FRONT

With 3mm (US 2) needles and C cast on 55(59:63:67:71:75:79) sts.

Moss st row K1, [p1, k1] to end.

Rep the last row 13 times more.

Cut off C.

Join on M.

Change to 3.25mm (US 3) needles.

Beg with a k row work in st st.

Work 12 rows.

Dec row K to last 7 sts, k2 tog, k5.

Work 11 rows.

Rep the last 12 rows 5 times more, and then the dec row again. 48(52:56:60:64:68:72) sts.

Work straight until front measures 32(32:33:33:34:34:35)cm/12½(12½:13:13:13½:13½: 13¾)in from cast on edge, ending with a k row.

Shape armhole

Next row Cast off 4(5:5:6:6:7:7) sts, p to end. 44(47:51:54:58:61:65) sts.

Next row K to last 5 sts, k2 tog, k3.

Next row P to end.

Rep the last 2 rows 3(3:4:4:5:5:6) times more. 40(43:46:49:52:55:58) sts.

Cont straight until front measures 42(42:43:43:44:44:45)cm/16½(16½:17:17:17¼:17¼: 17¾)in from cast on edge, ending with a p row.

Shape neck

Next row K2, skpo, k to end.

Next row P to last 4 sts, p2 tog tbl, p2.

Rep the last 2 rows until 23(25:27:29:31:33:35) sts rem.

Work straight until front measures the same as back to shoulder, ending at armhole edge.

Shape shoulder

Next row Cast off 11(12:13:14:15:16:17) sts, p to end

Next row K to end.

Cast off rem 12(13:14:15:16:17:18) sts.

SLEEVES

With 3mm (US 2) needles and C cast on 69(73:77:81:85:89:93) sts.

Moss st row K1, [p1, k1] to end.

Rep the last row 13 times more, inc one st at centre of last row. 70(74:78:82:86:90:94) sts.

Cut off C.

Join on M.

Change to 3.25mm (US 3) needles.

Beg with a k row work in st st until sleeve measures 34cm/13½in from cast on edge, ending with a p row.

Shape top

Cast off 4(5:5:6:6:7:7) sts at beg of next 2 rows. 62(64:68:70:74:76:80) sts.

Next row K1, skpo, k to last 3 sts, k2 tog, k1.

Next row P to end.

Rep the last 2 rows 10(10:11:11:12:12:13) time more. 40(42:44:46:48:50:52) sts.

Next row K1, skpo, k to last 3 sts, k2 tog, k1.
Work 3 rows.
Rep the last 4 rows 3 times more.
32(34:36:38:40:42:44) sts.
Next row K1, skpo, k to last 3 sts, k2 tog, k1.
Next row P to end.
Rep the last 2 rows once more.
28(30:32:34:36:38:40) sts.
Cast off 3 sts at beg of next 4 rows.
Cast off.

BUTTONBAND

With right side facing, starting at beg of neck
shaping, using 3mm (US 2) needles and C, pick
up and k105(105:107:107:109:109:111) sts evenly
down left front edge.
Moss st row K1, [p1, k1] to end.
Rep the last row 20 times more.
Cast off in moss st.

BUTTONHOLE BAND

With right side facing, using 3mm
(US 3) needles and C, pick up and
k105(105:107:107:109:109:111) sts evenly up
right front edge to beg of neck shaping.
Moss st row K1, [p1, k1] to end.
Work 3 more rows.
1st buttonhole row Moss st 4, k2 tog, y2rn, skpo,
moss st to end.
2nd buttonhole row Moss st to end working twice
into y2rn on previous row.
Moss st 10 rows.
Work 1st and 2nd buttonhole rows again.
Moss st 3 rows.
Cast off in moss st.

NECK EDGING

Join shoulder seams.
With right side facing, starting at beg of neck
shaping, using 3mm (US 2) needles and C, pick
up and k27(27:29:29:31:31:33) sts up right side
of front neck, 6 sts down right side of back neck,
k34(36:38:40:42:44:46) sts from back neck hold
pick up and k6 sts up left side of back neck,
27(27:29:29:31:31:33) sts down left side of front
neck. 100(102:108:110:116:118:124) sts.
P 1 row.
Cast off.

SCARF

With 3.25mm (US 3) needles and C cast on 13 s
Moss st row K1, [p1, k1] to end.
Rep the last row until scarf measures 160cm/6
from cast on edge.
Cast off in moss st.

TO MAKE UP

Join side and sleeve seams. Sew in sleeves. Sew
on buttons.
Fold scarf so that one 'half' is 15cm/6in longer
than other half, with fold to centre of back neck
and longer half on right side, sew scarf to neck
edge edging.

YARN COLOURS

Midnight
101

Storm
102

Moss
103

Claret
104

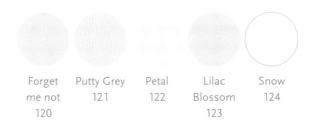

Forget
me not
120

Putty Grey
121

Petal
122

Lilac
Blossom
123

Snow
124

Scarlet
140

Grass
141

Daisy
Yellow
142

Fuchsia
143

Peacock
144

Fawn
160

Seaside
161

Plum
162

NDEX

NOTES

FROM MILLAMIA

We are so thrilled to be presenting you with our latest adult pattern book – only the second one we have ever produced.

We feel Colour Coded really captures the essence of the MillaMia design look that has helped differentiate our children's collections to date and we are now excited to be applying the same concept to adult patterns. What is equally rewarding is that many of the patterns in this book are relatively simple knits – they show that striking design does not always have to equal complexity or difficulty. In many ways they perfectly convey the ethos of Scandinavian design which is based on simplicity.

This was a fun book to work on – it naturally came together as a collection and Helena loved putting together these bright, vibrant colourways that we showcase in the photography. However we are confident that for those who prefer a more muted palette, the items within will be fabulous in those alternative colour combinations too. It would be great to see a Bella Cardigan in a sophisticated combination like Storm and Lilac Blossom for instance. The joy of the internet and sharing of projects on websites such as Ravelry means that hopefully we soon will.

When it came to styling the shoot we knew we wanted to capture an urban, modern "feel". The warehouse style of the studio we chose worked perfectly, as did the juxtaposition with the beautiful wallpaper we borrowed from Helena's talented friend Rachel Kelly's latest home collection. Rachel is a peer from Helena's student days at St Martin's College in London.

Helena knew that she wanted to balance the st. background of the studio with something prett more floral and more colourful and Rachel's wo immediately sprang to mind. In choosing the models we knew we wanted a mix of ages and looks to showcase the versatility of our designs Our team particularly enjoyed selecting the ma model for this shoot as you can imagine, but we have to say it is harder than you might think trying to select faces that you feel will not only work well individually, but also together and for a certain look. It made us all grateful that we ar not models ourselves!

The adult collections still feel fresh and new to us – a departure from our established kidswear designs. The response to our first collection 'Country Escape' was so fantastic that it has really given us confidence moving forward with this book. Our loyal customers seemed to like both our designs and the new format. Equally a thrilling has been the number of new customer that the adult collection has introduced us to. seems that the risk we took in making the jump from children's designs to adult patterns (in response to the overwhelming customer reque we had) was entirely justified.

We are delighted that we have a third adult boc designed and being prepared for later on this year (to be called 'High Society'). As Katarina has a baby due at roughly the same time Colou Coded goes to print we have had to be very organised to make sure that we have the third book ready before autumn also!

With best wishes,
Katarina and Helena Rosén
katarina@millamia.com or helena@millamia.co